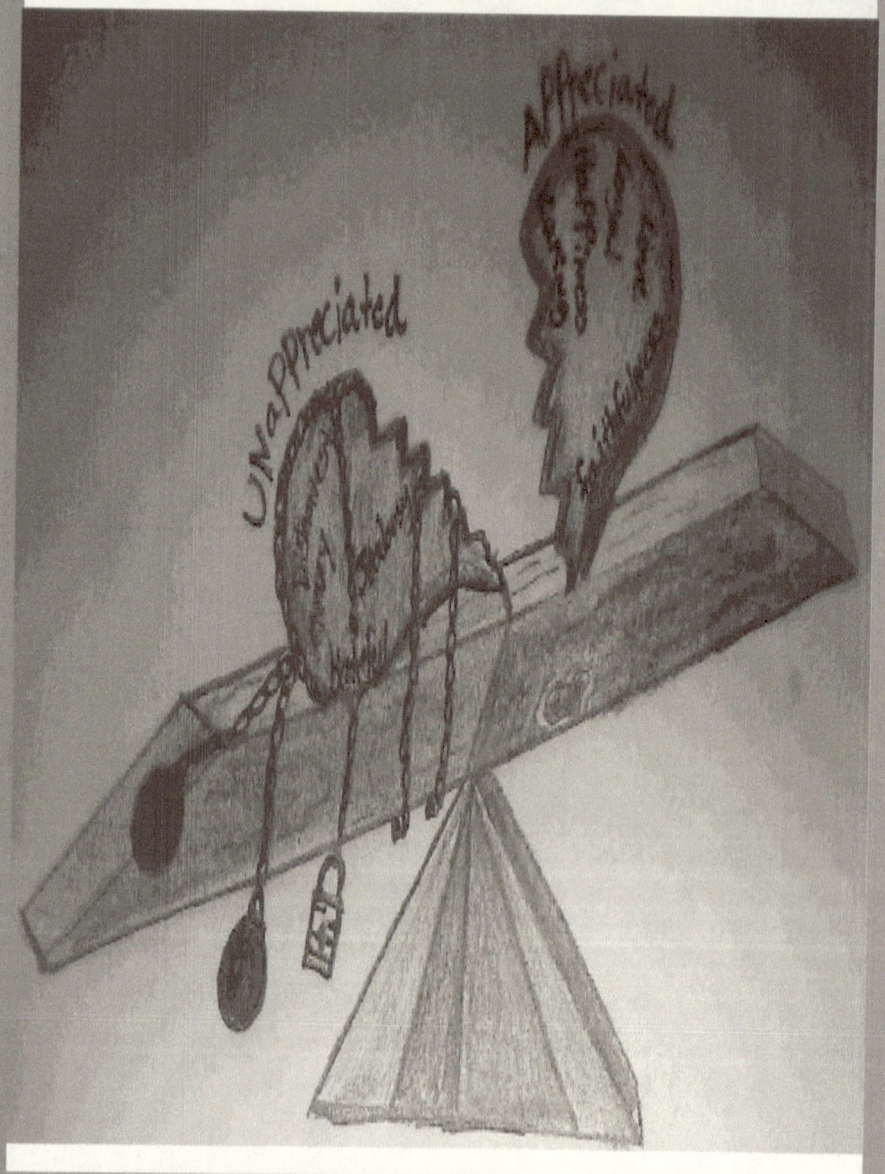

The Measures of Hate and Love

By: Nakiya Tate

Cover Illustrated by: Tyler Hill

Logo Designs by: Andre M. Saunders/Leroy Grayson

Editor: Anelda L. Attaway

© 2017 Nakiya Tate

ISBN 978-0-9988433-2-2

Library of Congress Control Number: 2017937680

All rights reserved. This book is protected under the copyright laws of the United States of America. This book may not be copied or reprinted for commercial gain or profit. The use of short quotations or occasional page copying for personal or group study is permitted and encouraged. Permission will be granted upon request. For Worldwide Distribution, available in Paperback. Printed in the United States of America. Published by Jazzy Kitty Publishing, LLC. Utilizing Microsoft Publishing Software.

PREFACE

This book was established through my thoughts and contents of life. The struggle of being loved, falling in love, love that is abusive and being hated by love. My personality is divine and my creativity is unique.

It seems so strange the way love works. You think you've found the right person and he or she ends up being Mr. or Ms. Wrong. In the process of finding Mr. or Ms. Wrong, you try to correct your wrongs to make them right. Your vision is blurry and your mind is rambling; but no matter what you must make your vision clear and get your mind to think clearly. You take in so much that you start to fight with yourself. You take so much until you do not want to show your face.

Love hurts most of the time. Love can stab you in the back, love can knock you down, but you get back up and try again.

After the third time the game is over. Three strikes and love is out the picture. Three strikes and you are not a winner. I measure the hate that attacked me then, but I measure the love that dwells within. The dimensions of hate are a mixture of torn emotions and trying to find my way.

Looking back, I can say that things have been in the dark, things have never been said out loud. Why do I write? Because it frees my mind and deep down inside. Life is like a flower when it does not get enough food or water it dies. When you feel dead, when you are alive that is when you must look at yourself in the mirror and ask the question, WHY ME?

Through the struggle, the anticipation, and fear I always knew God was near. Even when I questioned Him and yelled at Him, I knew he would one day come through.

When I look in the mirror, I reflect on what has happened; the relationships that went bad, the friends that turned their back on me, the family that put me out or threw me to the wolves. I also think about the nights I cried myself to sleep.

How does a young person get rid of all the animosity?

How does she live through all the torture and low self-esteem?

How does she stop the feelings of not wanting to live, feeling that nobody loves her anymore, or even the feeling that some people were out to get her?

How does a young girl that is trying to find her way make it each day?

How an elementary child can turn into a high school teenager and then after that becomes a college student just to end up back home without finishing school. Um...All the things I have been through I can go on and on. However, years after all that, I've come out strong.

At the end of the day, I found my Mr. Right. He said I stalked him, but I am no stalker. This is my dimension of true love, the connection, the bond; the hearts that intertwine was all a part of my Mr. Right. He spoils me since he loves me; He makes me happy when I am sad. We have our ups and downs and greatest of all, the ups always outweigh the downs.

Relationships matter, but you must love yourself first. Relationships can break you or build you with a hard grip. It is up to you to love yourself and be the one to know if you are in love or if it is Pure Damn Lust.

Lust is a sin if you didn't know it. In fact, it's one of the 7 deadly sins. I was lustful for a long time, but then God opened my eyes and I found the true meaning of what love was about. I found the true meaning of what love really was, now I can make some sense of it. I hated to love because love hated me. Now, I am in love because of love. Yes love; loves me back.

ACKNOWLEDGMENTS

I thank God for my gift of writing and that He guided me through this process.

A special thank you and gratitude to Anelda Attaway and the Jazzy Kitty Publishing Staff for making my dreams of a published author to come true!

DEDICATIONS

This book is dedicated to the Lord, my Heavenly Father, God Almighty, and if I had to choose three words, I MUST choose I Love You! You gave me life, good health, and strength to carry on. Thank you Lord for the opportunity to express myself. You loved me when I did not even love myself.

To Marcel Tate, the Love of My Life. Our bond is stronger than anything. God put us together because He knew what the outcome would be. He knew that we will make a difference in life. Thank you for believing in me and sharing all the sentimental and significant events in my life. I love you with all my heart!

To my beautiful daughter, Ki'yanna Loveina! The first day you came into my life, my world changed forever. You're almost 3-years-old, and the beauty of watching you grow daily makes me feel like the greatest mother in the world. God has blessed me with more than enough and I am so thankful to have you in my life. Your smile lightens up my dark world, your hugs melt my heart, and your kisses warm my heart. I love you with everything in me. My Baby Girl, you will always be forever! Mommy loves you beyond measure.

To my first Godchild Gianni; I love you and cannot wait to spend more time with you.

To the lovely women that have been in my life for YEARS! Thank you for putting up with me. Thank you for loving me and allowing our friendship to grow into something nobody could ever destroy. God placed each of you in my life for a different reason. I keep you close in my heart. Each of you know who you are so, smile because if you think I am talking about you, I am. I love you and God bless you always.

Last but not least, to my friends and family! Thank you for the support. Thank you for being there and having my back when you did. Thank you for the love. God bless each of you.

TABLE OF CONTENTS

INTRODUCTION i
Part I – Reflection: "I'm Looking at Self" 01
   Bold and the Beautiful 02
   Desire to Dream 03
   Who Hides Behind the Face?!? 06
   Getting from Give Me to Make Me 07
   It's More to Me then What You See 11
   Don't Give Loyalty unless it's Earned 13
   My Other Half 14
   The Promise 16
   Doing the Right Things 20
   A Whole New Kinda Bubble 23
   Notice 25
   Thoughts 28
Part II – Family and Friends: The Relationships within Hate & Love 32
   Consideration 35
   I Forgive 37
   Block the Attack 40
   Put Me Out 41
   The Family 43
   The Family II 44
   Sisters 47
   The Struggle 49
   Say No 51
   Even Though 54
   I Think I Know 57
   The Heart 59

TABLE OF CONTENTS

Where Are You God? 61

From Me to You 63

The Friends 66

A Friend 68

The Bound 70

Pick and Choose 72

Part III – Love Abhorred Me: The Relationship that Despised Me 73

Love 75

Love is Blind 76

Love is Too Blind 78

Copy and Paste 80

Tryin 81

Recovery 87

Suicide 89

In the Wrong 92

In the Wrong Once Again 95

Crying Out for Your Love 96

Never Know 98

Wanted Me Back 101

This Time of Nite 104

You Told Me to Wait on the Other Side 108

He's Just Like the Rest 110

I Should Have Known 112

The Other Girl 115

Ma Feelinz R Gone 117

The Words You Say 118

TABLE OF CONTENTS

- The Way 119
- Tossin' and Turnin' 122
- Why Me? 1244
- There Were Times 1255
- Wonder 127
- Stuck on Love 129
- All I Need is You 130
- Love is My Past 131
- I Will Be 132
- When I Close My Eyes 133
- Part IV – Love: Love, Loves Me Back 134
  - Just a Thought 136
  - You 137
  - The Unborn Child 141
  - Reading My Status is an Option: Letting Her in is a Blessing 146
  - The Life, The Seed and The Blessing 149
  - Beauty 151
  - You are the One 152
  - Mr. Right 153
  - Take Me Places 154
  - Picture Me 156
  - I Know You Really Love Me 158
  - Brown Eyez 159
- ABOUT THE AUTHOR 160

INTRODUCTION

Love can make you do imprudent things. Love can make or break you, not knowing what it is meant to do. The people you love are close to you, precious to you and more. No matter if it is family, friends, or a lover. When I say 'lover' I mean a spouse, a boyfriend or a girlfriend.

What is love?

What is love intended to do?

What is love all about?

What is the meaning of love?

When we realize how to love or whom to love, our heart will beat 10 times faster than normal. There are different kinds of love.

Family is **F**unny, **A**mazing, **M**ature **I**ndividuals Who **L**ove **Y**ou. Well, that is what FAMILY means to me.

Friends are **F**unny, **R**ich **I**ndividuals with **E**nergy, **N**ice, **D**ear, and **S**weet. This is what FRIENDS should be to me.

People will hate you, people will love you, but it is up to you to love yourself. Finding disappointment in people is the last thing you would want to do. For LOVE is a 4-letter word. Love is intended to Care, Motivate, and Commit to whatever you believe in.

Part I - Reflection:
I'm Looking at Self

BOLD AND THE BEAUTIFUL

Believe me I know it's True

Every day is a Blessing

Angels watch me Day and Night

Use your FAITH to **Trust God More**

Trust Me, I know I will be there with you

Imagine God WHISPERING in your Ear

Everything is Alright

Fight with Love

Usually Ask and Pray, it Works!

Love and Be Love

Because Life is Beautiful

DESIRE TO DREAM

Standing in the Window

Day Dreaming of Life

And Everything It Means to Me

So, Precious

So, Pure

So, Sweet to my Senses

I ask God, is it my **Desire to Dream?**

Is it my **Desire to Dream?**

To Dream about Life

To Dream about who will be in it

To Dream about Love

Happiness and Fun

Is it my **Desire to Wonder?**

If love Loves me

Is it my Desire to Feel?

If love Cares

Is it my **Desire to Imagine?**

What my Dreams will be

When they came True

They WILL Soon Come True

Is it my Desire to Dream?

Life always seems questionable and dishonest. When it comes to self-esteem and love we always have questions. When it comes to love we always need answers.

If you think about who you are and what you are; what do you see? What do you know about who you are? All I ask is, who hides behind this face?

WHO HIDES BEHIND THE FACE?!?

Attracting, Good Looking, Style polishes with Gloss, Fairness, and Good Looks all within Beautiful person
WHO HIDES BEHIND THIS FACE?

Take off, Outbreaks, A Fresh Start to Come
WHO HIDES BEHIND THIS FACE?

Good Nature Cheerfulness, Great Humor and Lite Heart
WHO HIDES BEHINDS THIS FACE?

TRUTHFULNESS
WHO HIDES BEHIND THIS FACE?
FAITH
WHO HIDES BEHIND THIS FACE?

IMPOSSIBLE VAIN EXPECTATIONS

A DEAD DUCK THAT'S WHAT

**BUT STILL,
WHO HIDES BEHINDS THIS FACE?**

GETTING FROM GIVE ME TO MAKE ME

Realizin' when I Pray

I ask God to give me This and That

Bless me with This and Bless me with That

Hardly EVER ASK to Fill my Personality

Or

To make me a NEW Individual in Him

To make me a BETTER Person in Him

To help me to UNDERSTAND my Struggle

It was like I Worried...

Worried about what People had to say

About me and my Relationship

I Destroyed So Badly

I wanted to be ACCEPTED

Doing that, I tend to MISS my Destiny

Had to hear HIS VOICE

Had to part myself from Love

NO LUST

Walk by Faith, NOT by Sight

I had to Fight with FAITH
Never knew When and Where
How or Why God did it
GOOD THINGS come to them WHO WAIT

WAIT ON JESUS, you see
God loves Me MORE THAN I loved Myself
How can you love, when you don't love YOU?

After a while, I spoke LIFE inside of me
I spoke LOVE inside of me
I spoke PEACE in my Heart and Soul, Realized
HAPPINESS comes When BITTERNESS GOES

It's NOT about Me ANYMORE
The JOY of the LORD is My Strength
Now, I have to get out of my COMFORT ZONE
Things can't go my way

I asked God, What I shall do?

I want to be Closer

Give my ALL to You

Getting from Give Me to Make Me

HE WILL ALWAYS MAKE A WAY

It's time for me to STOP ASKING

And JUST DO

It is it for me to STOP ASKING

Have to Ask God to make me A BETTER PERSON

Have to ask God to help deal WITH GRAPPLES

Overcome the Circumstances

Time to get out the COMFORT ZONE

Had to find My Way ON MY OWN

Getting from Give Me to Make Me

Lord Fill my PERSONALITY

Make me PURE

Make me PRECIOUS

Make me who You CALLED Me to Be

I will have a BETTER PERSONALITY

THANK YOU IN ADVANCE

EVERYTHING you Promised me

I THANK YOU IN ADVANCE

I give You a YET PRAISE

All I Have is my PRAISE

PRAISING YOU IN ADVANCE

IT'S MORE TO ME THAN WHAT YOU SEE

Never know **WHAT** God has **IN STORE** for you

WOW

Don't look like THE PAST

Don't look like WHO I'VE BEEN WITH

Nor Do I look like Trials and Tribulations struck me

WOW

Don't look like THAT NEGATIVE OUTCOME

I MADE IT

I made it through THE STORM

HE MADE A WAY OUT OF NO WAY

Delayed MY BLESSING, **But hasn't Denied It**

In Progress to get my Blessings -

To Reach MY DESTINY

How can I MOVE FORWARD...

When I DWELL on my PAST?

My past will not last,

Cus I'M LOOKING in the FUTURE

He ELEVATES me to PROGRESSION

To get to the NEXT DIMENSION

I have to ACCEPT the Little Things

IT'S MORE TO ME THAN WHAT YOU SEE

DON'T GIVE LOYALTY UNLESS IT'S EARNED

Faithful, Trustworthiness, Sincerity, Reliability,

Honor, Support, Zeal, Honesty

Obedience and Dependability

All defines LOYALTY

A person who is Characterized

With such Classifications

What does it mean to be Loyal?

You CAN'T give Loyalty

To humans WITH NO HEART

When one is Sad…

Do you Share your Heart?

Or

Turn away

Don't give LOYALTY <u>unless</u> it's Earned

Loyalty is a Powerful Characteristic

MY OTHER HALF

OH WOW!

HOW?

It's another me

What next?

You know TOO MUCH about me

Where were you at…

When I couldn't even think twice?

I found **the OTHER HALF OF ME**

But wait…Is it too Good to be True?

The OTHER HALF OF ME

OH NO

IT'S JUST ME

Looking in the Mirror

I found the OTHER HALF OF ME

As you grow, you never know who will be next to you. You never know how God will do what He promises you.

When you make a promise, it is meant to be kept, it is meant to be honest and true. People make promises, but are they meant to be broken. Are they meant to be misunderstood? She made a promise.

THE PROMISE

A Bird **Promised** She would FLY

A Rabbit **Promised** She would MOVE

At a STEADY PACE

A Young Lady **Promised** to STAY CLOSE

To HER MOTHER

BUT...

She **Promised** to LOVE HARDER

She **Promised** to LOVE MORE

She **PROMISED** to LOVE with ALL HER MIGHT

She **Promised** to BE THERE for HIM

THROUGH IT ALL

She **Promised** that <u>before</u> She takes his HAND

In MARRIAGE

She will Prepare herself to LOVE HIM

And Make him HAPPY

She **Promised** to HOLD HIM DOWN
She **Promised** She would FLY with HIM
And <u>knew</u> She COULDN'T Fly

She **Promised** to WALK NEXT to HIM
She **Promised** to LOVE HIM MORE
She **Promised** to MOVE with HIM
She **Promised** to LOOK FORWARD to the FUTURE

She **Promised** to be HAPPY and STAY HAPPY
She **Promised** to MAKE IT WORK
She **Promised** to TELL HIM EVERYTHING
NO MATTER WHAT

She **Promised** to SAY WHAT'S ON HER MIND
She **Promised** to PRAY to GOD for EVERYTHING
She **Promised** to be the BEST SHE COULD BE
She **Promised** to LOVE GOD and LOVE HIM TOO

She **Promised** to make this **Promise** to him that...

WE WILL LIVE HAPPILY EVER AFTER

A RING Can Tell a Story

A Story that will NEVER Grow Old

The Measures of Love and Hate

Sometimes I think of life and all the things in it. You never know what grapples may come your way because you cannot see in the future. The times you think of excitement in your life, you want to make sure things are right. I think about my life and I want to know that am I doing what is right.

DOING THE RIGHT THINGS

I find myself Sitting Here

Sitting in the Days

Often Wondering...

Where I went Wrong?

It is SO HARD making Decisions

Especially if they are Right

Knowing people want you to do

SOMETHING ELSE

It is SO HARD Trying

Trying to PLEASE other People

Trying to PLEASE Family

And making them Happy

It is SO HARD Trying

Trying to make YOURSELF Happy

All at the same time

Where did I go Wrong?

I live life RIGHT,

But just now how everyone EXPECTS it to be

I live my life the BEST I can

And life seems to HURT ME ONCE AGAIN

I find myself ALONE

I find myself CONFUSED

I ask myself, What is Best for me?

Your bubble has not popped, but there are still rocks being thrown at you and you do not know what to do.

You look in the mirror and see your world crashing down. At the end of the day, you have to realize that you can and you cannot fail; only succeed. And you cannot give up, only persevere. Giving up is not an option.

A WHOLE NEW KINDA BUBBLE

Looking at your Life outside of a **Bubble**

It's like a piece of **Bubble Gum**

When it gets TOO BIG it Pops

Your Life can be like this **Bubble**

Your Life can be BIG

With Riches and Gold

But with God...

It can be Wealth and Pure as Gold

Don't need to be Rich

To live Life to the Fullest

God is that Whole New Kinda Bubble

When Life seems STRANGE

Don't Explode

It's just that **Bubble** that has to Pop

But this **New Bubble**

Will NOT Pop

Because it's **a Whole New Kinda Bubble**

GOD'S BUBBLE IS HUGE

NO ONE CAN POP IT

NOT EVEN Blow it Up

That Bubble that Sits in your Chest

'YOUR HEART'

It can only be DESTROYED by You

NOTICE

I sit in a Dark Room with ma so called Girls

All they do is Gossip…

WOW

They Talk about everybody else

But their Lives are NOT FULLY together

What is that all about?

I sit in the Room

I Notice I'm sitting in a Corner

Not paying attention, IN MY OWN ZONE

Wondering and Thinking 'bout Life

Thinking about Who's in It

Thinking about Who Cares

The Good People-NOT many

It's just NOT A Part of Me Anymore

The things they do DON'T INTEREST me

I Sit by Myself

And I see MORE LIGHT in the Room

What is the difference?

I find myself on another Level,

I find myself Higher in God

I find myself Closer to God

And the things I use to do I don't do anymore

To be continued is Engraved on my wall…

It means…A NEW LIFE for me

It means the things that I do

Now affect the one that is Close to me

The things that I say now Affects

The one that I Love the Most

I can't find that Romance in me

I can't find that Sweet in me

I can't find that Good in me

At the time, I couldn't find anything Good in me

Go to Church and go Home

Do the same things ALL OVER AGAIN

When God started Dealing with me

I seen Reality

Watching as Well as I Pray

I don't say much anymore

Sitting Back and Watching

God Promised EVERYTHING would be Okay

Taking ONE DAY at a Time

Letting me know how to make the Right Decisions

Listen God told me

Those who Laugh

Laugh Last

The First shall be Last and the Last shall be First

I gotta get my Stuff Back

I Noticed the difference in me

I am a NEW Being

THOUGHTS

Today is Another Day

I sit Here and Write what's ON MY MIND

Just these THOUGHTS

I can't seem to get Rid of or Hide

It's like my Mind is Tortured

By the Thoughts in my Mind

I put my Head in the Sink

Thinking the Water will Erase my THOUGHTS

I'm Frozen

I CAN'T Move

Thinking about the One I Loved the Most

My Mouth dry

My Eyes are Dry and Itchy

I'm Gasping for Air

My Lungs closed up

NO ONE there to Help

I Fell to the Floor

And can't CRY because I Died

1, 2, 3, 4

It took Four Long Seconds

To try to Breathe ON MY OWN

But it did not work

I looked to the Sky and I seen an Angel

WOW GOD

Save Me and Gave Me HIS HAND

He took my Hand

And He gave me Strength

He took my Head

And gave me Knowledge and Wisdom

He took my Body and gave me Love

And Gave Me Peace

HE SAVED ME ONCE AGAIN

I ask myself WHY

Why ask myself Why?

Why do I Write out my THOUGHTS

I tell myself WHY

I Fight with my THOUGHTS

I Fight with my Guilt

I Fight with Emotions, Lies, Hurt, Pain,

And Self esteem

It all Tugs at me

Is that Why I Write?

I Express my Feelings

I Express my Pain

To know that I Love You

With NOTHING to Do

To know that I don't know…

Which Way to Go

Confused, Disappointed

Cus I know I STILL Love you

But I Love JESUS MORE

Just a matter of being on Top of the World

Waiting and Waiting and Anticipating

I Sit in the Light

Thinking about you

And the Next TENTH of a STEP

I can only IMAGINE…

If I'm being **Thought** about

With these Thoughts in my Mind

I can only Say

I know he is *NOT* thinking about it

Part II - Family and Friends: The Relationships within Hate & Love

When you fail, you try again and again until you succeed. Persevere not for them, but for you. Grapples may come and go, but it is only a test to make you stronger. How can you have a testimony if you never experienced a test.

You look in the mirror sometimes you may see failure, but you have to motivate yourself to make things right. Fight for what is right. You try to recover, but only God can help you heal. I fought myself day in and day out, but at the end of the day, I could not win. So, I had to ask God to fight the battle.

When you think of family you think of closeness, good memories, joy, and peace. When you think of family you do not think of hatred, envy, jealousy and strife.

What happened to the family? Everyone is distant.

What happened to the family? Nobody gets along.

What happened to the family? Friends are good to have when family seems to not care; your friends are there to stand in the gap. Friends come and they go;

however, God will make it just right and put people in your life that is meant to be in your life. Sometimes we have to separate ourselves to grow and be humbled to hear what God is telling us for our own good. Can anyone imagine the pain, hurt, and lies? All I can say is relationships matter.

CONSIDERATION

A form of Respect and Thoughtfulness

When someone is Hurt by Words

A Family member or Friend

You ask the question…Are you Okay?

Do you need to Talk?

If you need me, I am Here for you

NO ONE is **Considerate**

But every time I make sure I am

NO ONE seems to **Care**

NO ONE seems to **Care about my Feelings**

But I make sure I Do

Even if it's just something Small

Even if it's just a little Fall

I make sure I'm there to Catch you if I can

I make sure Everybody is Okay

I drop EVERYTHING I'm doing to make Sure

Everything is Okay

Can anyone be Considerate?

I FORGIVE

To FAVOR her Vexes me

There is NO getting around it

You make her seem like she is the ONLY One

You have Six and IT'S NOT FAIR

TWO are a Pain, so you say

ONE you DON'T Deal with

ONE you HARDLY ever see

And ONE you DON'T SEE AT ALL

I Love you ALWAYS no matter what

Please Pardon Me

It's just the Way I Feel

My Emotions are just getting to me

I have ONE and she is my PRINCESS

You only CALL when you NEED something

Do you EVER ask am I Okay?

Or How was my Day?

How are you Feeling?

What do you wanna Talk about Today?

How have you Been?

Do you EVER ask me THAT?

I Love you MORE

Because it makes me STRONGER

God OPENED the Doors

There is NO Stress NO Longer

To FAVOR her Vexes me

There is just NO getting around it

The Measures of Love and Hate

You know the family can love you one minute and hate you the next. When you need them the most they are the ones to put you down. Even when they help you they always want something out of the deal. Instead of loving with their hearts, they tend to love with their heads. I do not understand it, but it is a true fact. If they had a heart they would reach out and help, but now you see family can be your worst enemy…

BLOCK THE ATTACK

Humble yourself, He will do the Rest

Strong Holds come Across me

They try to Challenge me

I have to get Rid of the enemy

Demons try to face me

Block the Attack with a Shield from God

Block the Attack and Knock the enemy Down

Be Humbled

And God will SURELY do the Rest

PUT ME OUT

Five months Pregnant I WALKED to Work
Good Exercise is the Key-Right?
I try NOT to ask for Help
UNLESS, I REALLY NEED IT

Before I go to Sleep I Cry Late at Night
I don't know where I will End Up
-Think I liked Sleeping on the Couch
NO NOT AT ALL

All in All,
I tried my BEST to go to Work to Provide
The Couch was Uncomfortable
So, I go and get an Air Bed

Man, was that a Problem
I thought that would Solve a Problem
Well now, it's in the way
Sunday and here the Drama begins

Can I Wash my Face First?

Brush my Teeth?

NOPE!!!

SHE SAID I CAN GET OUT

Well...Where is all this Coming from?

Pregnant and Alone

Wow...How could she do this?

Whelp...I knew it was Coming Soon

THE WAY SHE TREATED ME

How can she Act Like She Likes me there?

Talking about me Behind my Back

Instead of Telling Me How she Felt

Hum...I didn't Understand that

Whelp...I know now

She was Putting Me Out

THE FAMILY

Family is MORE than just a Word

Behind **FAMILY** there is

Love, Joy, Happiness, Fun, Cries and Laughter

Behind it there is You, Me, Mom, Dad

Sister, Brother, Uncle, and Aunt

I'm forgetting Niece and Nephew, Cousin and Friends

Can you picture that?

Behind **FAMILY** there is

Hatred, Envy, Jealousy and Strife

And Sometimes Torture

But most of all the kids will say,

That's not Nice

Family is MORE than just a Word

We stand in the Gap or just Uphold **the Family**

THE FAMILY II

Growing up I Loved you

I Loved the things we USED to Do

I Cared and Imagined my Life as a Plan

Growing up Matured me

Graced me and Gave Me Faith

What is it today?

Family is just a Waste

You Regret the things you Did

You Regret things you NEVER Did

You Regret the things you WOULD HAVE Done

Some things you just can't Change

Now you Opened your eyes to see the Actuality

To Understand that **Family** is MORE than just a Sketch

Of that Symbol in a Storybook

It's MORE than just a Word

But **Family** is Separated

Family is Destroyed

Until someone CAN ADMIT their Faults

NO BONDING-NO LOVE to Share

Where is the Family?

Family is just a Waste

But with Faith

We will be Saved by God's Grace

Sometimes it is so hard to help people. It's like you stop everything that you are doing to tend to someone else, but if you are in a jam it is like stones have been flung at you. Sometimes even the ones that are close to you seems to kick you under the bus, stab you in your back and then some. When it's all said and done, you still love them with everything you have, with you whole heart and soul. You try to do everything for them, but they still end up letting you down.

Sometimes it is so hard to please the family. No matter if it is good, you still get talked about, you still get shut down. But God will not shut you down, will not stab you in the back, nor will He be two-faced and talk about you behind your back when you say NO. That is what is wrong with the family today, we can't seem to get along because of the petty things. We can't seem to get along because of the "he said, she said" like we are random people off the street. Consider the love that is still in my heart even though it's been hard to deal with the stress and hurt I still manage to forgive.

SISTERS

We Fight

We Argue

At the End of the Day,

We are There

We don't see Eye to Eye sometimes

We Disagree a lot

At the End of the Day,

We are There

Who can come Between us?

The enemy has before

Who can come Between us?

A man has before

Who can come Between other so called

Family members?

People come Between us

Can I Live with the Hurt?
Or Just Let It Go?
Can I Dwell on the Past?
Or Should I Let It Go?

Should I think about the Good?
Or Do you think it's Worth it?
Should I think about us together?
How Life would be Perfect

The Good times, The Bad times
We always come together

What ONE **Sister** to do without her
Other TWO **SISTERS**
I CAN'T IMAGINE IT

THE STUGGLE

It's like a Generational Curse

Lord TAKE IT AWAY

TAKE IT AWAY

It's like a Chain Reaction

Lord TAKE IT AWAY

It's like a Fungus that Keeps Growing

No Good Outcome to Grow In

The Love is Disappearing

Where is the Help?

The Support and the Hope

Where is the Love

And the Joy that Comes in it?

Where is the Care?

All I see is a Burden

Burning me Inside

No One to Help me to Survive
God, where are You?
It's like a Generational Curse
Everybody out to get you

Where is the Responsibility?
Where is the Honesty?
Lord TAKE IT AWAY

It's like a Generational Curse
We should have Billions
Helping each other Seeing Eye to Eye
Sticking together like Glue

Where is the Love?
The Joy and Happiness and Fun Too

Where is the Outcome of Good to come?
Lord Help Us break this Generational Curse

SAY NO

I say NO not to Hurt you

I say NO cus I DON'T see you Trying

You Say you want to Do Right

But I DON'T See it

You Say you want to do This and That

Please JUST Show it

I don't want to KNOCK you Down

I Love you MORE than Anything

I want to see you Succeed

I want to see you Doing Ya Thing

I want to see you on Top of the World

I want to see you Where You Want to Be

I don't want to Hurt you

I can't BECAUSE I Love you

I mean EVERY Word

Cus it's Eatin' up My Insides

I'm NOT losing Sleep

Stressing Over some other Issues

I have my Own to Deal with

I will Help in all ways I can

I don't think it's Fair to Try

Again, and Again

When we got Nowhere

I don't think it's Fair

When I DON'T see, you Trying

I don't think it's Fair

But you know I Really Care

It's NOT just me Anymore

I have to Weigh My Options

I have do what is BEST For All of Us

I don't wanna have to Let You Go

I have to BECAUSE I Love you

I'm Tryin' to Deal with All of This

But if I Thought about Everything

I will be in an Institution Locked Down

With Straps on My Arm

Locked Down FORCED to take Medicine

I don't want that, I have a Family

I Support my Family

You are Family

I tried to Help

I TRIED

What else is there to do?

But to Say NO

And Let You Go.

I'M SORRY

EVEN THOUGH

You may not BELIEVE the Words I say

You may not think I Care

You may not Believe me

But I know What is True

I can't Judge you

Only Help you

I can't Take it Any Longer

But it will ONLY make you Stronger

The way you have a GREAT Sense of Humor

The way you have a Great Heart

I know God WILL make a Way

Sometimes it is Best to Stand alone

To see what God has for you

To see what God will Do

I know you may not Believe me

But I know what is BEST for you

Stand alone and Trust God

HE WILL SEE YOU THROUGH

Sometimes family thinks they know what is best for you. I look at the mistakes they have made as I was growing up. I always told myself I did not want to be like anyone in my family. Not saying they are bad people, just the decisions they made and the way they treated each other. How can you love outsiders more than you love your own family? How can you give advice when you cannot take your own advice in the meantime? In some cases, I think I know what is best for me.

I THINK I KNOW

Been through So Much, so many Hard Times

Call me Strange,

Call me Weird

Call me WHATEVER comes to your Mind

I know Where I'm Going

Some Amazing People see you Doing Well

Try to Break you

Or Knock You Down

God knows my Heart

He knows What I am Doing

He knows Where I am Going

To be Happy is a Joy

To be Happy is a Delight

To be Happy is a MUST for Me

Years wrapped up in a State of Depression
Years wrapped up in Sadness
Years lost in Darkness and Didn't Realize it
Now, I think I'm on Top

I think I know What I am Doing
I think I know Where I am Going
I think I know What God has for Me
I think I know Who God has for Me
I think I know that God Created me for His Purpose
I think I know I am a Special Woman

Through it all I know the Road is NOT always Easy
Through it all, I know that there will Bad Days
Through it all, the Good WILL Override the Bad

I know how NOT to Complain
I know how to Count My Blessings
I know how to NOT take things for Granted
I know how to Live

THE HEART

When you Argue it Hurts me to my **Heart**

When you Fight that Hurts me to my Soul

When you DO NOT see Eye to Eye

I don't want to be Around

The Resentment towards the Sisters

The Belittling from the Mother's mother

Wow how all have Fallen a part

Can't Bare the Pain, the Torture on the Inside

I try to Grow up and Put it all Behind

I see my Life as Sweet and Divine

There is TOO MUCH on My Mind

The Back Stabbing and Betrayal

I thought it was FAMILY

When I think about it, it Sickens me

The Hatred, the Envy and all the Jealousy

The Resentment towards the Sisters
The Belittling from the Mother
Can't Bare the Pain, the torture inside

I try to Put It Behind
I see my Life Sweet and Divine
There is TOO MUCH on My Mind
LORD FIX **THE HEART**

WHERE ARE YOU GOD?

When I Cry Out for the Family

Where are You God?

When I thought it got Better

I DIDN'T see You God

The Thought of Everyone getting Along

It sounded Great

The Prayer of Healing Relationships

Where are You God?

The thought of You Whispering

EVERYTHING is Okay

I BELIEVED You God

When I had Little Faith

I COULDN'T see You God

When I asked You to Breathe on the Family

I asked, How could You God?

How can You Breathe on People…

That DON'T wanna change

What can You do God?

Oh Ye of Little Faith

He said Trust in Me

Oh Ye of Little Faith

He said Believe Me

Oh Ye of Little Faith

WATCH ME DO IT

I AM HERE

FROM ME TO YOU

I Loved you since we were Kids

We've been Best Friends since Day One

You know we Always had each other's Back

I Love you with all my Heart

You know I'm Always Proud of you

It was like Yesterday

We were Riding Bikes together

It was like Yesterday

We were Sitting on the Green Box

Having them Long Conversations about Life

I Vent to you

Cried to you cus I Knew you did the Same

It seems like Yesterday

We were in Diapers

Now, we can make our Own Decisions

Tears Low

I can't Believe we are all Grown Up

Now, we can find out who we Really Are

No matter what I'm Always Here

Even when you have Too Many Tears

Friends come and go; at the end of the day, the ones that stay are the ones that you hold on to. Good friends are hard to come by. Even when you live and go from one chapter to the next chapter in your life, you realize the friends you use to have and the friends you have now are the ones that are meant to be in your life.

Growing up your parents always said to choose your friends wisely. Friends are important and they can share great memories throughout life. The ones you have today are in your life is for a reason. No matter if they are near or far, they will always be considered friends no matter what.

THE FRIENDS

I notice that FRIENDS Come and Go
The ones that Mean the Most
STAY IN YOUR LIFE

The Hatred, Gossip, and Jealousy you NAME IT
Who wants to be ASSOCIATED with that?

Even if I haven't talked to my FRIENDS in Months
We Call every ONCE IN A WHILE
Have a GOOD Conversation
Knowing that you Miss them

Knowing that if we DON'T Call
For another THREE MONTHS
It will be Okay

If you ALWAYS Think about them
NO MATTER WHAT
It will be Okay

I Love MY FRIENDS

They are MORE than just FRIENDS to me

They are Like my FAMILY

They are FRIENDS to Hold On to

I'm THANKFUL for the FRIENDS I have

A FRIEND

I only known you for

A SHORT Period of Time

We grew Together

And Understand each other

I Hear your Story

It TOUCHES me

Because your Story is SIMILAR to Mine

When I Look at you

I see Courage

No matter what TRIES to Break you…

You Snap Back and Grab it

BEFORE it Grabs you

In your Eyes, I see Hurt

Hurt that NEEDS to Heal

But your Life is like LAYERS that has to Peel

The Hate is Burning ALL INSIDE

Because someone had to Lie

The Waste of Time was NO Waste

Because a BEAUTIFUL Blessing

Came out the Deal

The Loyal Friend I know you are

The Strong Woman I know you are

The Independent Woman I see makes you strong

The Beautiful Mother who has a Warm Heart

I know you do the Best you can

It will get BETTER just Watch and See

God Bless a Beautiful Friend

THE BOUND

We STICK Together

They take you in as their Own

They Love You Better

Care for you Better

Spend Time with you More

Appreciate and Admire EVERYTHING

You Do

Treat you like a Person

Honesty is the BEST Policy you know

Honesty will ALWAYS Show

They Understand

They care with Open Arms

They Save me

They MADE SURE I had

I Appreciate and Value our Friendship

We make Ends Meet

We Mend our FEELS

If we have a Falling Out

We Share our Thoughts

We Forgive and Forget

Love and Move on

That is a true **BOUND FRIEND**

PICK AND CHOOSE

Tugging between THIS Friend and THAT Friend

How can I Decide?

They DON'T care for One Another

How can I Decide?

When I LIKE Both of Them

They DON'T WANNA Hang Out

With Each Other

Tugging between THIS Friend and THAT One

Setting Dates to Spend Time together

Trying to find out WHEN they are Free

Hanging Out with Her

And Eight Plus Three

Hanging Out with THIS One and THAT One too

How can I CHOOSE

When they MEAN?

Part III - Love Abhorred Me: The Relationships that Despised Me

Lust is one of the seven deadly sins. When you are so wrapped up in "love" you do not think nothing of it. You find yourself in love and that is all you know.

When you think, he loves you but he is just using you.

When you think, he cares but he just wants you to work so he can take your money.

When you think, the relationship is perfect and there is still something missing, but you just cannot fathom it.

Even though love is a two-way street, It was just a one way street. It was just fast love falling into lust. You never know what men intensions are to wanting to be with you, but at the end of the day Mr. Wrong was NEVER right for me.

LOVE

Passionate, Attraction, Compassion, and All

Souls INTERTWINE that's the Reason

I'll make you Mine

Together Forever, the Time is Near

LOVE IS EXALTED

Lips COMPRESSED together

We standing in lovely Snowy Weather

Comparing the **LOVE** to the Sweetest Kiss

To Adore the ONE, I TRULY Missed

Attached is a **LOVE LETTER** Devoting the Vowels

The Preacher ask NOW Are You Ready?

You may Kiss the Bride

Thick and Thin is TRULY ALIVE

Make it Happen

BECAUSE our **LOVE** is Compassionate

LOVE IS BLIND

I sit in the MOON LIGHT thinking at Night

Wondering what to do Next

I realized I can't take NO MORE

Thinking about you Day in and out

This is not how it's Supposed to be

In the Morning

I get up NOT READY to Face the Day

The Heartache, Pain, Guilt and Hurt

But when I Close my Eyes

I Dream of ANYTHING Possible

When I Open my Eyes

I just seem so Sad

I don't think about the Past

I'm just Focused on RIGHT NOW

LOVE IS BLIND

It can't be Defined

I Smile to Erase the Pain

I Smile to Erase the Hurt

It just don't Work at all

Life is going in Circles

I'm ready to make a Change

LOVE can't be Defined

LOVE IS JUST TOO BLIND

LOVE IS TOO BLIND

Hey
You SAID you Love me
What does Love mean?

You SAID you are Here for me
What is the Meaning of that?

LOVE IS BLIND to you
It don't Mean a THING to you

When I'm Happy, you MAKE me Mad
What is the Meaning of that?
Maybe I will NEVER Understand
LOVE IS TOO BLIND TO SEE

It's an Action-YOU KNOW
Show me that you Love me
Show me that you Care
Show me that you will Always Be There

Words don't MEAN a thing

Love don't MEAN anything

If you don't show me that you MEAN it

COPY AND PASTE

I Love you

So, I **COPIED** my Heart

So, the Love wouldn't Fade away

I **PASTE** the Feelings BACK into Place

But it all just Erased

WOW, I don't know

Can I press Undo?

Can I Undo the Relationship?

Or should I just Delete it?

Man, it's hard trying to **Copy and Paste**

This Relationship Back together

Man, it's hard trying to Undo what we had

Man, it's hard to Delete the Past

Copy and Paste all of my Memories Just Erased

TRYIN'

Constantly havin' a DREAM

Of you Lying NEXT to me

I OPENED my Eyes

You're Gone in the morning Dew

You Fade away like an Imagination

Like a Cloud in the Sky

The Day we Talked and Talked for Hours

Kissed me so PASSIONATELY

I thought that was the day

I fell Deeply in Love

I couldn't Resist the Temptation

God didn't Allow me to go Far

I asked myself WHAT HAPPENED

How in Months we grew Apart

I thought I had EVERYTHING Together

But you were Gone

From under my Nose

I Anticipated and Pondered

On the Future to come so Fast

I Wondered what it would be Like if he was…

Erased OUT my life Forever

Can't accept the fact it Happened

Made Mistakes and took things Out on You

But the TRUTH is there

There was just something Wrong with me

I see why Good Men are HARD to find

I see why Women LOSE them Fast

But too it men Can do the Same

Put everything Together

And there's NO Lookin' Back

Put Two and Two together

And is NO Goin' Back

The Measures of Love and Hate

I Burned that Year So Deep Within

Didn't want to Remember the Past

Brings to MANY Tears

It Kills me on the Inside

But NOW, I cannot Hide

Constantly Dreamed of You Lying NEXT to me

Was Missing the late-night Calls

Missing the Late Nights…

When we SPENT time Together

I can anyone Let Go

If someone said they Loved, you

What happened to Forgiving

One Million and Tenth MORE Times

What happened to Loving Forever

Loving someone is Harder than you can Imagine

Love STAYED and it STRAYED away

Loving him was Pain
I didn't know if I would
Talk to him Again

Friends just didn't Work for me
Would that be the Last Time?
If it was MEANT to be
Then it will Be and Last

Copying signs of Love, Emotions
And all of his Feelings to my Heart
I hurt MORE and MORE
The way it was it Shouldn't have been
The way it happened Couldn't have been

God HELPED me Up when I was Down
I was Weak
But this only Made me Stronger
I was Weak and STAYED Weak for a while

I Closed Myself In, Stayed in the Dark

I know it is Real, felt like I Lost my Dog

My Best Friend

Or Even my Better Half and All

It's like a building a House with NO Roof

Having a Shoe on and Forgetting to put a Sock on

Trying to Find the NEXT Light

Riding a Bike without one Tire

The One I Loved meant MORE than Anything

I thought you had to Lose someone

To Get Them Back

I thought if I Hurt him

He couldn't Hurt Me Back

Connected like the Cable to the Cable Box

Connected like the Internet to the Computer

They worked Together very well

It's like Connecting Love to the Relationship

Connecting the Heart to the Other One

It's like Connecting the Lips to the Other

And Connecting the Eyes to his Eyes

I want to CRY and DIE inside

I see what I Use to See

I see what I Use to Feel

I see what I was Missing all over again

Trying to Get OVER you

RECOVERY

Restoration

Resurrection

Trying to Become Me Again

Trying to Become a better Woman of God

Trying to Become a better Woman PERIOD

Restoration

Resurrection

God, I Hear You and Trust You

Trying to Become a Wife to Be

I know it's not Meant to Be

Trying to Become a better Daughter

A better Friend

A better Sister

Trying to Become a better Aunt

I am not a Mother

Trying to Process this **RECOVERY**

Sometimes it is hard to think straight when you have so much on your mind. It is hard to move forward when your mind is cloudy.

Love can hurt you so badly, you have bad thoughts in your head. Love can hurt you so bad, it will have you doing horrible things. One thing that didn't last long was true love because love hated me badly. Love can hate you so badly you do stupid things and don't even realize it.

What can you do to make it right? Only you can figure the real love out.

SUICIDE

I COMMITTED **Suicide**

With my Heart and my Mind

The thin Line between Love and Hate

Could not be DEFINE

Suicide was on my Mind

The Lustful Emotions and attacking Desire

There was NO Love

So, I broke the Wire

Never thought my Mind

Could be so **Suicidal**

It took a TOLL on me

I COMMITTED **Suicide**

With my Heart and my Mind

I put my Mind to it

And thought about the Love

I was Careless, Unworthy and Useless

I left my Past and didn't want it to Last

So, I tried to make it to my Future

I was Stuck and I didn't want to Last

I was Stuck by Love

Love so Passionate

By love so Constant

By love so Heavy

Love so Endearing then all of a Sudden

I felt you Disappearing

I COMMITTED **Suicide** with my Eyes

All the Lies and TOO MANY Cries

What was I to Do?

But get away from you

Suicide was a Lie to my Heart and my Mind

I woke up from a Nightmare

But you were ALWAYS Right there

Suicide was an Illusion

But was SO Confusing

Now I Bruising

And found my Love, I'm Misusing

Taken by the Best

I got that off my Chest

Now, I'm Living in Regrets

Suicidal Mind and Lying All Behind

What is all that Now

I have to Admit it

Suicide was all in my Mind

IN THE WRONG

I can't Express it to the World
Maybe it's NOT meant to be
Only God can Judge me

Getting in the Relationship
Started out Great
Perfect-Too GOOD to be True

I ask myself-
Why women have a Habit of Running…
The GOOD MEN Away

If a REAL Woman Loved him
Things wouldn't have got that Bad
Doing the Little Wrong

We sit Down and Talk
BEFORE it becomes something Big
Hard to say Why I did what I Did

I knew that was the Child in me

I found Myself STILL in my Childish Ways

I found myself NOT FULLY Grown

I NEVER thought it was that Bad

I ask God to Mend this Broken Heart

The things I Did and Said

You would have Thought it was the Man

Not a SO-CALLED Woman

Who takes the Blame

But the Child that is being so Lame

To make a GOOD MAN Stray away

To make him Leave his Comfort Zone

To Push Him Away til he fell Overboard

What was he Supposed to do?

But go off to make it Bad

I was SO Childish

Things Can't go your Way

When you're in the Wrong
When you Mess up so Badly
He STARTS to Hate me

How can I tell if he STILL Loves me or Not?
When he Puts up with All my Mess

He GIVES me SO MANY Chances
He FORGIVES me SO MANY Times
I CAN'T Count How Many Times

IN THE WRONG ONCE AGAIN

People Watch and Start Waiting

To see you Mess Up AGAIN

They NEVER see what goes on Behind Closed Doors

I HATE myself More

Knowing I did someone so Wrong

I was in the Wrong

I took Love for Granted

Played with Emotions and More

How can he Love Me after that?

I want him to Love Me Back

It was a Lessoned Learned

I Experienced what I ALWAYS wanted to know

Why do women Push GOOD MEN Away?

I don't ever want to be in the Wrong

CRYING OUT FOR YOUR LOVE

I Wish you were right Next to me
I asked myself How This Could Be
I didn't Wish this on Anybody
How could this Happen to Me

I Count the Success in my Future
I know ONE Fame is You
I know I've been Stupid
Some things can't Hit you like Cupid

I can't Think so it's REALLY HARD for me to Blink
I Stare in Space while my Heartbeat Race
I get on my Knees and ask for Forgiveness

I get on my Knees PLEADING for your Love
Asking you to Love Me Again
To allow me Back in your Arms

I wanted you to Help me with things I Lack

I just want your Love again

To allow me Back in your Arms

On my Knees BEGGING for your Forgiveness

Wanting you to Love me Back

On my Knees ASKING you to Take me Back

Wanted you to Fill in the Empty sides of me

My Heart CRIES OUT for your Love

Can you Take Me Back?

I really have to Show it

Can you Take Me Back?

NEVER KNOW

You know you made Mistakes
Then you ask for Forgiveness
Not just from your Mate
But from God as well

When you know you are the One…
Who MESSED UP it is Bad
Someone shouldn't Take You Back

Even still they are Still there
Apart of them still Loves you
Being in Love can be a Task

Being in Love can be HARDER than it Seems
Being in Love you **NEVER KNOW**
What can happen UNTIL it Happens

It don't have to Planned
The Drama will just Land
Nobody thought it could be Me

The Measures of Love and Hate

Honesty, I must say

I was the Female to Push him away

I just wanted to do EVERYTHING Right

To do the Things he did to me

Make me Happy

Love me Beyond Measures

Love me MORE THAN Life itself

I couldn't Accept it, I wasn't Right Within

When it's TOO LATE to Realize what, you have Done

It's **too late** to Fix it

It wasn't Fair to Treat him that Way

But Learn from the MISTAKES you Make

Stuck in the Past is NOT a Good Feeling

When Love Hurts you

You Hurt Someone New

You try to Fix the Mistakes

Nothing Works

Don't want to be Stuck in the Past

Stuck in my Less

Stuck in all my Mistakes and Mess

If you **really** Love someone

Don't be like me…

Try to Work It Out

Are you Willing to Love Harder?

My Flaws made me Stronger

Can I Burn my Past?

Communicate, Understand one Another

Communication TORE us Apart

If you Love the way you Say

Then make that person Happy

You **NEVER** know what can Happen

WANTED ME BACK

After all that he **WANTED me Back**

I had to Find myself

I thought it was Love but Love is NOT Careless

Love will Love You Back

After all that

What was Difference now

That you **Wanted Me Back**

You Begged me and Begged me

Until I said NO I CAN'T

You Looked at me like a Puppy that Lost his way

You looked at me like Please Don't Go

He GAVE UP on me

Why would I **want another** Chance?

Maybe it was just the Things People Said

Maybe it was just the things I Heard about you

I didn't WANT you Anymore
After months of Hurting and Begging
I didn't NEED you Anymore

I PRAYED to God
And He HEALED me
Most of all He FORGAVE me
I didn't **WANT** that GUILT Anymore

The World can say what they Want
At the End of the Relationship
I was STILL in the Wrong
BUT YOU STILL **WANTED ME BACK**

My past was clutter. I found myself in a shell, but when I explored "love" I found myself in a mess. The thought of hating myself, and wanting to kill myself was a struggle. I thought it was love, but the enemy start to get the best of me. I tugged at it for a long time, but God saved me by his grace. Boys that think they are men, but do not know how to express themselves can hurt you badly. I thought finding a younger guy would be good for me, but It just hurt me more. I thought that exploring was best for me but all it did was hurt me. I was opened and vulnerable and for that I let feelings get in the way. Sometimes you have to experience something to find out if it is real or not. Love is not lust, but I thought it was. Can I grow up and become something more than just someone's play toy.

THIS TIME OF NITE

Guess I should be Sleep right now

Honestly, I CAN'T Sleep

All I do is Think of you

If I'm **not** Thinking I Dream

I take the Time to Write

What is On My Mind

I take the Time to

Write what my Thoughts are

Now, through next Week…

GUESS THIS TIME OF NITE

I would be sleepin' Right?

But not tonight so much on my Brain

Lookin' out the Window

It's Snowing pretty hard

I have to Admit

It's going to be a New and Refreshing year, "I hope"

I am Growing up, Twenty-one this Year

See just Sitting here

Writing what's on my Mind

Thinking about you

If I'm not thinking, I'm Dreamin'

Words can't even express the way I am feelin'

Rolled over lookin' at the Ceiling

The White Walls, and White Snow

White means Purity

Lord are You making me Pure and Whole Again

Mending all my Wrongs, Back to Right

Taking me to another Height

Taking me to another Dimension in Life

Making me Stand on my OWN Two Feet

Making me Stand Tall

Walkin' with my Head High

Instead of Low

This time of Night the Late Nite Calls

I just wanna Talk

And Curl up and All

But this Time of Nite now you Sleepin'

Take the Time

And ask me what I was Thinkin'

The Late Nite Calls and All

Use to make me Walk into the Sky and Fly

I sit in this Room Thinkin' about the First Time

In it I seen it Clear

I Wished you can be in it

Now, I'm Thinking that Nite was so Great

I wish we can Start OVER

And make it a Date

How I Miss all of it when it's Gone

What a Life Now

That things are not right Without ya

Realized he's Gone

Made me Think was it Meant to be

Realized he's Gone

Made me Think was it really Love

I didn't see myself going Anywhere

But I found myself Falling Apart

YOU TOLD ME TO WAIT ON THE OTHER SIDE

No-I thought you said you would Change

Are you worth my time?

I thought you said you would Change

I don't know why I Bother

You told me to *Wait on the Other Side*

You said, I am

But what about you?

I thought you said you would Love me

I know you just said That

Are you WORTH my Love?

Are you WORTH my Time?

Am I WORTH your Time

Or Am I WORTH your Love

Am I the One You Dream of

Day and Night

Am I the one you want to Meet

ON THE OTHER SIDE

Am I the one you want to See

ON THE OTHER SIDE

Why should I Wait for you?

Why should I Care?

Why should I take the Time to Love you?

Are you going to Show up?

Are you going to Love Me More?

I LOVE YOU

Do you Love Me?

I WILL WAIT FOR YOU

ON THE OTHER SIDE

HE'S JUST LIKE THE REST

U know-he just Said

He Loves me just to say it, Right?

It Sounds Too Good to be True

YEAH,

HE'S JUST LIKE THE REST

OH YEAH,

HE IS JUST LIKE THE REST

Sittin' here Laughing

Sitting here Shocked

Wow it's SO Amazing

HOW HE'S JUST LIKE

THE FREAKIN REST

Tell me the Same Line he told her

What that is CRAZY

But I dusted it Off and Moved on

I Opened my Eyes

I'm Good, He's Not

What is that all About?

OH YEAH

HE'S JUST LIKE THE REST

I SHOULD HAVE KNOWN

He was Younger than Me

Man, I was Weak

Maybe it was the First Things

He did to Me

After that it was a Lie

I knew the Truth

He trying to Front in front of his Boys

But I knew Right Then I was NOT a Toy

I have Emotions and Feelings too

To get Drunk and tell you…

How I Felt About You

I was a Fool

To Think that you would be Honest

I was a Fool

To Think that you Make Me Love you

Lustful Emotions and Lustful Ways

I was a Mess, but I Changed my Ways

I Thought I was in Love

How can I Love you?

When I DIDN'T even Know you

It's sad to Say it,

But Yes, it was Me

I know I was Messed up

Eight times plus Three

I tell you the Truth because…

Someone is Worse off than Me

I came to Reality to Find Myself Caught up

I came to Reality to Find our Love I Misused

I found that Lust I Reused

ALL OVER AGAIN

The Lustful thoughts

I Had about you

The Lustful things

I Wanted to do

I thought it was Love

But to find out it Wasn't

I SHOULD HAVE KNOWN

THE OTHER GIRL

I didn't know I was **THE OTHER GIRL**

He didn't Tell

But the Love I thought we Had

Was supposed to be Honest

The Love I thought we had

He was never Mad at me

It was too Good to be True

Too Good to Imagine

Too Good to Know if I was **THE OTHER GIRL**

A Year in and I thought it was Real

Well, I guess Youngsters…

Are Too Young Minded for me

I didn't look at the Fact…

He was a year Younger than me

But I gave him Encouragement

And it was Meant to Be

But he went Home

And I got a Phone Call

-WOW- his Girl

Actually, called to Confront me

I wasn't Afraid because I DIDN'T know

I just told her it's all good NOW, I KNOW…

They weren't together

So, I didn't Consider being **THE OTHER GIRL**

But in his Eyes, he still Wanted me

I didn't Understand that Part

He had a Girl

But at the End of the Day

I Washed my Hands of it

Cus I did not want to be **THE OTHER GIRL**

MA FEELINZ R GONE

KIYA-Wake up

Oh, I am up

I know it's NOT a Dream…This is Reality

MA TRUE FEELINZ R GONE

I don't Care, he Spit the same Lines

He Raps the same Verse

Oh, he is the Worse

MA FEELINZ R GONE FOR GOOD

Oh Yeah, he made me Mad as hell

I woke up and said,

"Only God can Mend a Broken Heart again."

He Spit the same Lines

And Rap the same Verses

Come to find out he is the Worse

Ha Ha Ha Ha, that is all I can do is Laugh

What is this Oh Feelinz don't seek the Truth

THE WORDS YOU SAY

The Words you say I Feel You Mean

The Words you say I Feel You Disrespect Me

The Words you say you have no Respect for Me

No Respect for God

The Words You Say

I Pray Even Harder

The Words You Say

I pray God has Mercy on You

The Words You Say

Make me want to Just walk Away

Is it Worth it

Is it Real

Is it Nothing

But a Heart made of Steel

THE WAY

I Lay Next to you

And Cry myself to Sleep

All I think of is how it all Bothers me

The Way you use to make me Smile

The Way you would make me go Wild

The Way you would Just Ask Me

If I am Okay

Or Even **The Way** you would Lean in

To Kiss me on the Face

The way I Try to Love You Harder

I Fall in and out of Love

I Lay NEXT to you

And Cry myself to Sleep

I Lay NEXT to you

Wondering if Everything will be Alright

I Lay NEXT to you

Praying Tomorrow will be Better

I Lay NEXT to you

Are you a Stranger I Lay NEXT to?

Sometimes "love" can kick you right in your chest and knock the breath right out of you. How can you deal with all of these issues love comes with? I still can't imagine the pain they put me through boys to men are they really in love with me? Seems like I still fight with my feelings, fighting with the lies and rejection love comes with.

How can I be so blindsided by love?

Love is a disease and now I am begging please, I don't want to love any more. Now, I'm begging please, take it away because I am not pure and I am unsure if love, loves me.

TOSSIN' AND TURNIN'

I Cry myself to Sleep
But that's NOT the End of Me
Tossing and Turnin'
What is Next with Me

I would feel Comfort
Instead I feel Low
What will make it Better
Only Time would Show

Wanting that Affection
And the Love that Comes with it
I Toss and Turn wonderin'
What LIES Ahead

In the next Chapter of my Book
Love hasn't really Struck
No, I don't need NO Luck

I got God on my Side

Because He is my Blessin'

I Toss and Turn

Because I have a Confession

Love has NOT Found me

But that is NOT the End of Me

WHY ME?

Sitting in Bed with you Next to me

I ask myself **WHY ME?**

The Way I want to Hate you

But God won't Let me

The Way I Love you

My Heart is Burning from you

Sitting in the Bed asking myself

WHY ME?

THERE WERE TIMES

When we had so much Fun

The times you would Call

And we Laughed and Talked

At One Point,

We Talked about the Future

What happened

I have NO CLUE

THERE WERE TIMES

We held each other Down

Told each other that we Loved One Another

But only Time would have Told us

If we Did or Not

THERE WERE TIMES

We Hung Out and had Fun

But those Times were NOT Real

I Loved you

Cared for you

And Told You Everything

But now I know

THERE WERE TIMES

We use to Share Everything

WONDER

I **WONDER** if I'm Happy

WONDER if I'm Sad

I just **WONDER** why I always make you Mad

To Look in your Eyes

I say I Love you

I **WONDER** if that was a Mistake

Was it a Front, a Test or just a Moment?

A Reaction

Or

My Heart really telling you

Is my Soul telling you the Same?

I think it was NO Mistake

I just wanna Go on this Date

Was I too Excited…I really Think So

Candy Kisses on my Mind

Our Hearts Shall Intertwine

WONDER what 25 Reasons why I Love you

I **WONDER** what Questions I want to Ask You Now

I **WONDER** what Life would be Like

When you Hold me Close to your Heart

The way I Think Will Change for a Lifetime

Will this Long-Distance Torcher Me Forever?

Amanda said it Just Right

God sent me an **angel**

Sent me an **angel**

To Heal my Broken Heart

But now, I CAN'T Feel you

"Now, I'm Begging God PLEASE

To Send You Back to Me

I can't Eat or Sleep

I took your Love for Granted"

What was that?

I just **WONDER** if it was Real

STUCK ON LOVE

STUCK ON YOUR LOVE

Addicted to you Badly

I Open my Heart with Joy and Gladness
I NEVER wanna Let you go Away
I NEVER wanna Let you go to Stay

I Love You More than Life Itself
I Love You More than Anything Else
I Love you, but I Love God More
I Love you with a Passion

I wanna Make you Mine
Will you Spend the Rest of your Life with Me?
I NEVER wanna Let You Go
NEVER wanna Let You Go far away to Stay
NO OH NO! EVER NEVER EVER!
I don't EVER wanna Let You Go far Away

ALL I NEED IS YOU

Those Times we were all Alone
The Times we ONLY had Each Other
Those Times we went through So Much
I DID NOT know What to Do

All I Wanted to Do was Love you
And Live my Life the way I Knew

All I want was the Best for Me and You
The Times I wanted you I did not know
I didn't know what I wanted at the Time

My Heart said Yes, but my Mind said I Don't Know
But all I know is I'm Tryin' to make it Right
For the Both of Us

We need to Share the Pain
We need to Share the things Left in the Rain
ALL I NEED IS YOU

LOVE IS MY PAST

Love is Behind me

At least I Thought

Lust is Erased now I am Taught

Respect comes a Long Way

Now and Forever

How about that you were the Lever

I thought I was the Bait because I couldn't Wait

But now, I know, Love is Behind me

Lust is Erased

Now, I am taught Respect comes a Long Way

Now and Forever

How about Now I be the Lever

You are the Bait cus now I can Wait

Cus Love is **My Past** and I knew Lust would

NEVER Last

I WILL BE

The Mother-Happy and Loving her Child
The Wife-Happy Loving her Husband
The Friend-Happy Helping her Friend
A Woman-Strong and Mending til the End

I want to be that Better Mother
I want to be a Better Lover or Wife
I want to be a Better Friend
I want to be a Better Woman

The Mother-Stressed Out
The Wife-Always Depressed
The Friend-Too Busy
A Woman-So Confused

I will be a Better Mother
I will be a Better Lover or Wife
I will be a Better Friend
I will be a Better Woman until the Very End

WHEN I CLOSE MY EYES

I knew that you were There

When I Gave you my Heart

I knew that you Care

When I Gave you that Hug

I knew that you Loved me

The way you Kissed me Back

I knew that we could Build that Life Together

When I Gave you my Heart

I knew that you would be There

When I Opened my Eyes

It Showed me

That there was No One There!!

Part IV - Love:
Love, Loves me Back

The Measures of Love and Hate

Being in love with someone can be a great thing. I told God I was done looking for love. I told God if he didn't send somebody my way, I was not looking because love always seemed to hurt me most. When I was weak it just knocked me far to the ground. When I felt like I couldn't get back up I felt like God had just given up on me. I felt like God didn't love me anymore. Why me Lord? I knew I was far off in the moment, I felt like walking off the face of the earth. But one day love smacked me in my face. Smacked me so gently it was like a cure it was like the sun rise on the ocean glowing next door.

JUST A THOUGHT

Candle Light Dinner

Roses around the Bed

Tender Kisses and Hugs to Share

Compassionate Touch ad my Heart Beat Racin'

When time comes Around, I Smile

You Show Me How MUCH you Care

Care about my Feelings

I am Happy

Now, I'm Living in the Next Chapter

In my Story Book

Happiness HITS me, Joy just HUGS me

God BLESSES me

You Shower all this Love

I Accept it

The thoughts in my Mind are they Real

YOU

YOU took the Time to Get to know me

Now **YOU** know TOO MUCH

YOU took the Time to get to Understand me

Now **YOU** Understand TOO MUCH

YOU took the Time to get to See what I see

Now **YOU** see TOO MUCH

YOU took the time to Care for me

Now **YOU** Care SO MUCH

YOU took the Time to Hold me

In a Time of Need

Now, **YOU** Hold me all the Time

YOU know How to Love me

YOU know How to Care

YOU know What to Say

Any Time of Day

YOU know How to Say it

The way **YOU** Make Me Feel

YOU make my Heart want to Heal

YOU are a Man of God

YOU know How to Pray

YOU know How to be Romantic

YOU know How to be Loving

YOU know How to be Caring

YOU

YOU are Kind

I know that **YOU** Care

I know that **YOU WILL ALWAYS** be There

YOU know that I'm Here

YOU know that I Love **you**

YOU know How I Feel

YOU know ALL About Me

YOU know I'm your Wifey

YOU know that I'm Emotional

YOU know that I'm your Friend

YOU know that I'm Someone

Special in your Life

YOU know

We are BOTH Blessed

I LOVE **YOU**

Because **YOU** know

The world seems to fade away when you face challenges each and every day. You look to Heaven and start to question God, or start yelling at God, but He comforts you in the meantime.

It is hard to face the challenges in life, but when God blessed me with a gift I could not give a way; I tested myself from that day on.

No matter what challenges come my way I will not regret any decision I make or any thought I have because now a beautiful blessing is the strength to my success.

THE UNBORN CHILD

I lay Looking at the Ceiling

I ask God, what is next in Life?

When is the Time I Start a New Life?

He just Told me to be Patient

I Respond with a lite Answer

Okay Lord

Closed my Eyes,

Thought I Heard her Call my Name

Cus she was Scared of the Dark

I Heard her say Mommy

I Heard her Cry

I Heard her say I want Daddy

I Understand a Daughter and Son…

Are Precious Gifts from God

To Sit and Say
She has to Have the World
I can only Imagine what God Placed
In my Heart

The Unborn Child
Has NOT been Conceived
Hasn't been Developed yet
Has NOT been Thought about

The thought came to Mind
But it NEVER Stuck to me
I always Told myself…
I was Too Young to Try

But to Dream of this Moment
Is a GREAT Feeling
But in Reality
I have NO Clue

I Sit under the Stars

As he Rubs my Stomach

Lay on my Chest to Hear my Heart Beat

To Kiss my Fat Checks

And his Love NEVER Changes

It makes Tears fall from my Eyes

Sit here and watch Maury every Now and Again

Mother's don't know Who the baby Daddy is

It Hurts me to know that

My Child is so Special

I can't Understand

WHO my baby Daddy is…

I don't want it to be like that

Laying here Dreaming of a Wonderful daughter

Waiting for her Daddy to come Home

From a long Day of Work

Pacing Back and Forth because I am so Miserable
I Sit and Dream One Day it WILL Come True

To Sit Here and Dream
That One Day it WILL Come True
It's a great Reason to think things Through

My nieces and nephews are my Bundles of Joy
So, I know it takes Courage to Raise them
They give me Energy, and Motivation
They give me Hope that my Future will be Great

The Unborn Child will have his Last Name
The Unborn Child will be the Seed of her Mother
The Unborn Child will be the Seed of her Father
The Unborn Child has NOT been Developed yet

This is a Dream…But it seems like Reality
I lay in the Hospital Bed
Because I had this Dream
I woke up Scared

Thinking, why did I have this Dream?

I asked God, was this Dream Real?

Was this just a Test?

A Test to take me where I wanted to Go?

He said that it was a Test

He said that I will Know when I was Ready

I will be a Queen

And I will find my KING

My Dream Will One Day Come True

The Unborn Child will be Reality

READING MY STATUS IS AN OPTION: LETTING HER IN IS A BLESSING

When I Carried her for the Eight Months…I did

I felt a Connection from Day to Day

The Time she was Conceived

To the Time she Developed Each Month

Till the Time I held her in my Arms for the First Time

I was TRULY Blessed

The Gift was in the Experience

Reading my Status is an Option

But Letting her in my World was NOT

She is my World

When I close my Eyes

I hold her Close to me

Our Heart beats

Beat together

We already Know each other

She Sparked my Heart

With so much Joy

She opened my Eyes to see Reality

She made me Smile harder than Ever

She made me Think about a great Future

Reading my Status is an Option

But letting her in my Life

Is the Biggest BLESSING I could ever Ask for

I am TRULY Blessed to have a Daughter

The Joy she brings me Every Day

She is already Strong

She has a Personality just like her Mother

I carried her for Eight Months

I knew I Felt the Love, the Bond and Joy

The Peace and Happiness came in

I Love her More and More

Loving the Joy of Motherhood

The Precious Moments

The Laughter and Smiles

She Sparks my Heart with all the Love

All the Joy and Happiness in the World

THE LIFE, THE SEED AND THE BLESSING

I Prayed for a Good Life

I Prayed for a Good Man

I Prayed so Hard

I Prayed so hard for the Right Things

The right Direction and Dreams

God Granted me all the Desires of my Heart

I decided what I wanted in Life

I NEVER Gave up

I NEVER Give up

God allowed me to Learn

He allowed me to Live

He allowed someone to Love me

Love me more than I Love myself

I love myself Unconditionally

More and More now I am Free

The Seed that Grew inside me

Was the Biggest Blessing for me

He Made, Created and Blessed it

He made a Way for me

He DID NOT look at my Flaws

Nor did he Judge me

He Looked at me and Gave me MORE Chances

More Chances than Ever

More than I can Count

On my Fingers and my Toes

Everything I asked for is a Blessing

I live with No Regrets

BEAUTY

Watching you Grow Amazes me

Allowing me to see the **Beauty** of Life Phase me

The **Beauty** of a Lifetime Praises me

I thank God more each day

Secure my Eyes to Dream of you

Walking, Talking, Jumping, Singing, and Laughing

I Dream of you saying a Million…

And one Word and then More

Imagine the way you Express your Love

Your Feelings and Emotions

You put a Smile on my Face

Embrace me with your Hugs and Kisses

You Bring Me Joy NO MATTER WHAT

BEAUTY is a song when I Think of you!

YOU ARE THE ONE

You are the One that makes me Smile

You have Class and too much Style

I want to be in it For the Love

Because I know it Comes from Above

MR. RIGHT

He Cares about my Feelings

He Cares about my Heart

He Loves me for Me

And Make sure he Gives me the World

He Treats me like his Queen

He is ALWAYS my King

He Holds me

Kisses me so Passionately

He makes me Smile

He makes me Happy

He makes me feel like a natural Woman

I am his Queen

I found my Mr. Right

TAKE ME PLACES

Close your Eyes make a Wish…

Stop, don't tell me

Make a Wish…

TAKE ME PLACES

NOT just Trips Around the World

But **TAKE ME PLACES** in your Life

Take me in Love

Take me in your Heart

Take my Lips and Comfort them with yours

Take my Arms and Wrap Them Back around you

Take your Hands and Put them on my Shoulder

Just being to say what's On Your Mind, I'LL LISTEN

Take my Love and Receive it

Pick up your Phone to Dial my Number

Let Ring Once and Hang up, Call Back

Just say I Love you and Hang up

Let me Mend ya Broken Heart

Allow me to Massage your Back

When you had a Long Day at Work

Rub your Feet cus you been on them all Day

Kiss you, Kiss you, Kiss you cus I Missed you

The way you Look at me

The way you Cook for me

Your wonderful Personality

You are ALWAYS yourself

Think Back at my Mistakes

And see how Far I've come

All the ones you could have Talked to

But you still Loved Me Regardless

Don't wanna be without you

Making all these Wishes

Most of them already Came True…Make me yours

I will live that Life of a Lifetime with you

PICTURE ME

PICTURE ME under the Moon
Holding you in a Tune
I asked God for this
And now, I'm Happy as can be

To Lay in your Arms and Sleep So Peacefully
To Open up to you and Try to get some Air

I allow myself to Stare in your perfect light brown Eyes
I Zoom into them and look Beyond your Mind
I Look into your Thoughts and Jump into your Dreams

To know that you are just a Phone Call away
To know that you are NOT Far away
Makes me feel Great

You will come Flying when I Call
Drop everything to come see what is Wrong
To Open my Heart to Accept your Love
To Picture us under the Moon and the Stars

Watching the angels Fly all Around

It is so Beautiful, can you Picture that?

Can you **Picture** us together Forever?

Can you **Picture** how life would be

When we are NOT Together?

How can you **Picture** the Bad with the Good?

When life is ALWAYS Misunderstood

Can you Picture that?

You once asked me...

What do I see when I Look in the Mirror

I would say I don't know

You would say look Deeper than the Black woman

Who been through so Much

And now, she is Out on Top

PICTURE ME in your Dreams

I Guess I'll know I'm NOT going Anywhere...

Can you Picture that?

I KNOW YOU REALLY LOVE ME

I haven't Talked to you in Weeks

But you Called me to Hear my Voice

You told me that you Miss me

My Heart lit up when you told me that you Love me

I KNOW YOU REALLY LOVE ME

You CAN'T go a Second WITHOUT me

I KNOW YOU REALLY LOVE ME

You Told me from Day ONE

I KNOW YOU REALLY LOVE ME

Because I Felt your Love DEEP WITHIN

I Love You Too

I KNOW YOU REALLY LOVE ME

From DEEP DOWN in your Soul

You Show me that you Love me

BECAUSE I LOVE YOU TOO

Brown Eyez

The way you Smile LIGHTENS Up a Day

The way you Talk Heals a Heart

You are you NO Other Man

1 million guys, but you are a True Man

I wouldn't have it NO OTHER WAY

I would have NEVER knew how Sweet you are

It's just a Time that I would have Experienced

Your **EYEZ** make a woman see the Beauty

Within your Heart

1 thousand Words is NOT ENOUGH

You have to Find What's Deep Down Inside

But what I want to know is could Dem

BROWN EYEZ really Lie

ABOUT THE AUTHOR

<u>The Measures of Hate and Love</u>:

A Poetry Book was written from deep within the roads of life. She traveled on a dark road trying to find her way, trying to find the true meaning of LOVE. She battled with low self-esteem until she looked in the mirror to find there is more to her than what she saw.

She fought for approval and acceptance, relationships with family and friends burned while others did not last. She battled with some disappointments and dishonesty but she started to find her way. She found the road not taken, the road to exuberance. She thought she found love but LOVE found her in reality.

She found the precise path and started to put the pieces back together to gain PROSPERITY. She gained LIFE so she can find PURPOSE.

Nakiya E. Tate

www.ingramcontent.com/pod-product-compliance
Lightning Source LLC
Chambersburg PA
CBHW021127300426
44113CB00006B/320